REFLECTIONS

OLIVE CROWE

ARTHUR H. STOCKWELL LTD
Torrs Park, Ilfracombe, Devon, EX34 8BA
Established 1898
www.ahstockwell.co.uk

ISBN 978-0-7223-4745-4
Printed in Great Britain by
Arthur H. Stockwell Ltd
Torrs Park   Ilfracombe
Devon EX34 8BA

CONTENTS

INTRODUCTION

Introduction   2016

I should like you to know how I came to compiling this little anthology. I recall visiting my grandparents almost a century ago, never being allowed to leave before taking out a 'promise' from a small box of tiny rolled papers – biblical quotes. Perhaps that's how this all started!

My mother taught my brother and me a prayer to end each day:

> *Lord keep us safe this night*
> *Secure from all our fears*
> *May angels guard us while we sleep*
> *'Til morning light appears.*

A well-known child's quotation with little or no meaning at the time, but more understood as time passed.

My father, polishing his very first car with pride, looked at me most seriously saying, "My girl, when you obtain something good, take care of it – with privilege comes responsibility and it will serve you well."

My school motto comes to mind – *Servite cum latitiae* – Serve with gladness – not a bad thought.

When I joined the Brownies at the age of seven, my still-long-time friend and I dancing round a toadstool (the mind boggles) very proudly quoted:

> *I promise to do my best*
> *To do my duty to God and the King,*
> *To help other people every day,*
> *Especially those at home.*

In my late teens, upon my baptism, words were quoted which to this day I recall with awe:

> *Be faithful unto death*
> *And I will give you the crown of life.*

Later when meeting my first and only boyfriend we discovered that not only was our favourite hymn 'The Day Thou Gavest', but we both enjoyed quotations, he himself writing poetry and prose which included this:

There is no mind but possesses some beautiful thing - pictures, memories from childhood giving not only form and colour but movement, scent and sound -

The ripple of a lake at sunset, the scent of rosemary, lavender or thyme, the voice of the sea, the wind in the tree-tops - tender voices telling of love, victory, eternity.

And it is his artwork and music that enhance these Reflections.

At our wedding Len and I both chose that I should walk in to the lovely hymn 'Praise My Soul the King of Heaven', which includes the quote:

Fatherlike He tends and spares us;
Well our feeble frame He knows;
In His hands He gently bears us,
Rescues us from all our foes.

Something that came to mind time and again in later life!

Another chosen hymn contains meaningful and helpful words:

Wherever He may guide me
No want shall turn me back;
My Shepherd is beside me,
And nothing can I lack.
His wisdom ever waketh,
His sight is never dim,
He knows the way He taketh
And I will walk with Him.

Here I should like to give you a brief résumé of how we experienced that guidance and wisdom from a most unusual happening to Len when he was just coming up to his fourteenth birthday in 1939. It happened like this: Len was dashing into a baker's shop for a loaf of bread when he was literally knocked off his feet by a large gentleman, who picked him up and after that kindly presented him with a business card with the possibility of 'a job in the BBC'! From this moment in time Len's first career began. He started as a pageboy in the library of Broadcasting House for the princely sum of fifteen shillings a week plus clothing allowance of two shillings and sixpence.

Time came for a few years in the RAF, training in radar. This proved a most useful asset on his return – this time to Alexandra Palace, where television was just emerging – and he became involved in outside broadcasting. Thereafter he experienced a most interesting and rewarding career in the expanding world of electronics engineering.

Upon early retirement Len felt called to study for the

priesthood and was ordained at Chichester Cathedral followed by a happy time as Vicar of Fairlight in East Sussex, Rural Dean of Rye for a time, and further service at many surrounding churches until, at the age of eighty-one, he had to relinquish the work he loved in his second career due to the beginning of dementia. But even then in his very caring nursing home he tended to get others to join him in singing:

> *Busily doing nothing,*
> *Isn't it just a crime?*
> *I'd like to be unhappy,*
> *But never do have the time.*

And they hear indistinctly at night:

> *As I lay me down to sleep*
> *I pray thee, Lord, my soul to keep*
> *And if I die before I wake*
> *I pray thee, Lord, my soul to take.*

So even reaching the end of his life Len still has quotations somewhere in there – in his heart and on his lips – even if he does not know it.

We have enjoyed sharing our lives with a very loving family – now including three grandchildren and eight great-grandchildren, together with nephews and nieces and an enormous number of friends – so very blessed!

From the family I have gleaned these snippets of quotes and reflections:

Miriam & Andy

I could never myself believe in God if it was not for the Cross. . . . In the real world of pain, how could one worship a God who was immune to it?

John Stott, reflecting on suffering and the Cross

Linda & Terry

In all your ways acknowledge him and he shall direct your paths.

Proverbs 3:6

Nathan & Sarah

There is nothing nobler or more admirable than when two people who see eye to eye keep house as man and wife, confounding their enemies and delighting their friends.

Homer

Lorna & Dan

We turn to God for help when our foundations are shaking, only to learn that it is God who is shaking them.

Charles C. West, professor of Christian ethics

Hannah & Simon

Every saint has a past and every sinner has a future.

Oscar Wilde

All this in time has given me the urge to share with others a number of reflections that I trust may be of some help to you at some period of your life and I trust that God will bless you as much as he has blessed Len, myself and our lovely family and many friends over the years.

Olive Crowe

LOVE

There are three things that last for ever: faith, hope and love; but the greatest of these is love.

1 Corinthians 13:13

God so loved the world that He gave us His only begotten Son, that whoever believes in Him shall not perish but have eternal life.

John 3:16

Life is only for love; time is only that we may find God.

St Bernard

God is love.

1 John 4:8

God loves each one of us as if there was only one of us to love.

St Augustine

No one has ever seen God, but if we love one another God lives in us and His love is made complete in us.

1 John 4:12

We cannot know whether we love God, although there may be strong reasons for thinking so, but there can be no doubt whether we love our neighbour or no.

St Teresa of Ávila

Jesus said: By this shall all men know that you are my disciples - that you have love one for another.

John 13:35

For I am convinced that neither death nor life, neither angels nor demons, neither the present nor the future nor any powers, neither height nor depth nor anything else in all Creation will be able to separate us from the love of God that is in Christ Jesus, Our Lord.

Romans 8:38–39

There is no pit that God's love is not deeper still.

Corrie ten Boom

Love wasn't put in your heart to stay; love isn't love till you give it away.

Song

To love the whole world for me is no chore.
My only real problem is my neighbour next door.

C. W. Vanderbergh

God made me, God loves me, God keeps me.

Dame Julian of Norwich

Work is love made visible.

Kahlil Gilbran

Love's secret is always to be doing things for God and not to mind because they are such very little ones.

Fred W. Faber

Keep on loving each other as brothers – do not forget to entertain strangers for by so doing some people have entertained angels without knowing it.

Hebrews 13:1

Often, often, often goes Christ in the stranger's guise.

From a Celtic poem

The sacrifice of freedom is the paradox of love.

Studdart

Be still and know that I am God.

Psalm 46:10

Thou hast made us for Thyself and the heart of man is restless until it finds its rest in Thee.

St Augustine

If a Christian has to change his plans it is always because God has something better in store.

Phil Webb

You can give without loving, but you cannot love without giving.

Amy Carmichael

Feel for others - in your pocket.

Charles H. Spurgeon

Our Lord does not care so much for the importance of our works as for the love with which they are done.

St Teresa of Ávila

Help one another with encouraging words.

Romans 14:19

A gentle answer turns away wrath, but a harsh word stirs up anger.

Proverbs 15:1

I hold it true what e'er befall –
I feel it when I sorrow most –
'Tis better to have loved and lost
Than never to have loved at all.

Alfred Lord Tennyson

Grief is the price we pay for love.

Dr Colin M. Parkes,
quoted by Queen Elizabeth II
after bombing of Twin Towers.

The Cross is the only ladder high enough to touch
heaven's threshold.

G. D. Boardman

Our Lord has written the promise of the Resurrection, not in book alone but in every leaf in springtime.

Martin Luther

Seven wonders of the world: to see, to hear, to touch, to taste, to feel, to laugh, to love.

A student, when asked to list seven present-day wonders of the world

The King of Love my Shepherd is,
Whose goodness faileth never;
I nothing lack if I am His
And He is mine for ever.

Henry W. Baker

You never so much touch the ocean of God's love
as when you forgive and love your enemies.

Corrie ten Boom

God gives us love.
Something to love He lends us.

Alfred Lord Tennyson

When the Holy Spirit controls our lives He will produce this kind of fruit in us: love, joy, peace, patience, kindness, goodness, faithfulness, gentleness and self-control.

Galatians 5:22

The faithful love of the Lord never ends. His mercies never cease.

Lamentations 3:22

Love does no harm to its neighbour: therefore love is the fulfilling of the law.

Romans 13:10

The greatest thing a man can do for his Heavenly Father is to be kind to some of His other children.

Henry Drummond

Friendship is the nearest thing we know to what religion is. God is love – and to make religion akin to friendship is simply to give it the highest expression conceivable by man.

Henry Drummond

FAITH

In the beginning God created the heavens and the earth.

Genesis 1:1

We do not need a great faith, but faith in a great God.

Hudson Taylor

I believe the Bible is the best gift God has ever given to man - all the good from the Saviour of the world is communicated to us through this book.

Abraham Lincoln

What is faith unless it is to believe what you do not see?

St Augustine

Faith does not operate in the realm of the possible. There is no glory for God in that which is humanly possible. Faith begins where man's power ends.

George Muller

God has created me to do Him some definite service; He has committed some work to me which He has not committed to another. I have my mission - I may never know it in this world, but I shall be told it in the next. I am a link in the chain - a bond of connection between persons; He has not created me for naught. I shall do good. I shall do His work. I shall be an angel of peace, a preacher of truth in my own place, while not intending it, if I do but keep His Commandments.

Therefore will I trust Him wherever, whatever I am - I can never be thrown away: if I am in sickness, my sickness may serve Him; in perplexity, my perplexity may serve Him - He does nothing in vain. He knows what He is about. He may take away my friends, He may throw me among strangers, He may make me feel desolate, make my spirits sink, hide my future from me - still, He knows what He is about.

John Henry Newman

Faith is greater than learning.

Martin Luther

True faith is ever connected with hope.

John Calvin

You can only see well with the heart: what is essential is invisible to the eyes.

Antoine de Saint-Exupéry

Jesus Christ - the same yesterday, today and for ever.

Hebrews 13:8

Jesus said: I am the Way, the Truth and the Life - anyone who has seen Me has seen the Father.

John 14:6–9

I am the Resurrection and the Life - those who believe in Me, though they die will live.

John 11:25

Jesus said to His disciples: Because you have seen me you have found faith. Happy are they who never saw me and yet have found faith.

John 20:29

God moves in a mysterious way
His wonders to perform;
He plants His footsteps in the sea,
And rides upon the storm.

William Cowper

I do believe; help me overcome my unbelief.

Mark 9:24

Faith builds a bridge from this world into the next.

Anon

We walk by faith, not by sight.

2 Corinthians 5:7

So we fix our eyes not on what is seen, but on what is unseen – for what is seen is temporary; but what is unseen is eternal.

2 Corinthians 4:18

In Him we live and move and have our being.

Acts 17:28

I believe in the sun even when it is not shining. I believe in love even when I feel it not. I believe in God even when He is silent.

Words found on a cellar
wall in Cologne after
the Second World War.

I am not skilled to understand
What God has willed, what God has planned;
I only know that at His right hand
Is One who is my Saviour.

Dorothy Greenwell

He is to be seen in the light of a cottage window as well as in the sun or the stars.

A. Clutton-Brock

Jesus said: Whoever hears My word and believes in Him who sent Me has eternal life And will not be condemned – he has crossed over from death to life.

John 5:24

Nothing is or can be accidental with God.

Henry W. Longfellow

Real true faith is man's weakness leaning on God's strength.

D. L. Moody

Be faithful unto death and I will give you the crown of life.

Rev. 2:10

I will meditate on all Your works and consider all Your mighty deeds.

Psalm 77:12

The world is not lacking in wonders but in a sense of wonder.

G. K. Chesterton

The heavens declare the glory of God; and the firmament sheweth His handywork.

Psalm 19:1

Angels help us to adore Him;
Ye behold Him face-to-face;
Sun and moon bow down before Him,
Dwellers all in time and space.
Alleluia, alleluia!
Praise with us the God of grace.

H. E. Lyle (Psalm 19)

He has made everything beautiful in its time.

Ecclesiastes 3:11

I praise You because I am fearfully and wonderfully made - Your works are wonderful - I know that full well.

Psalm 139:14

Surely God would not have created such a being as man, with an ability to grasp the infinite, to exist for only a day! No, no, man was made for immortality.

Abraham Lincoln

Faith draws the poison from every grief . . . and quenches the fire of every pain; and only faith can do it.

Josiah Holland

Faith gives substance to our hopes, and makes us certain of realities we do not see.

Hebrews 11:1

Yea, though I walk through the valley of the shadow of death, I will fear no evil: for Thou art with me.

Psalm 23:4

I know that my Redeemer lives, and that in the end He will stand upon the earth.

Job 19:25

I am the Alpha and the Omega, the First and the Last, the Beginning and the End.

Revelation 22:13

Christ has died: Christ is risen: Christ will come again.

Book of Common Prayer (Communion)

I have to believe that God's in control, and for me to always demand answers is to assume His role. I have decided to sit back and let Him be God and let me be me

Phil Cooke

How good is the God we adore,
Our faithful unchangeable friend,
Whose love is as great as His power
And knows neither measure nor end.

Joesph Hart

Now to Him who is able to do immeasurably more
than all we ask or imagine . . .

Ephesians 3:20

PRAYER

More things are wrought by prayer
Than this world dreams of.

Alfred Lord Tennyson

Prayer should be the key of the day and the lock of the night.

A proverb

The world we build tomorrow is born in the prayers we say today.

Dr Jonathan Sacks

O most merciful Redeemer, Friend and Brother, may we know You more clearly, love You more dearly and follow You more nearly.

Richard of Chichester

The place for prayer is everywhere.

John Blanchard

Prayer is the key to heaven's treasures.

John Gerhard

I have many times been driven to my knees by the utter conviction that I had nowhere else to go.

Abraham Lincoln

Life is fragile - handle it with prayer.

Anon

I'm tired, Lord, but I'll lift one foot if You will lift the other for me.

Sadie Patterson

When life beats you to your knees you're in the best position to pray.

Tony Miles

Time spent in prayer is never wasted.

François Fénelon

Prayer from the heart can achieve what nothing else can in the world.

Mahatma Gandhi

Pour out your heart to Him, for God is our refuge.

Psalm 62:8

The desire to commune with God is intensified by the failure of all other sources of consolation.

Charles H. Spurgeon

It is possible to move men, through God, by prayer alone.

Hudson Taylor

If you wish to find out the really sublime repeat the Lord's Prayer.

Napoleon

Our Father who art in heaven,
Hallowed be Thy name.
Thy kingdom come.
Thy will be done on earth, as it is in heaven.
Give us this day our daily bread.
And forgive us our trespasses
as we forgive those who trespass against us.
Lead us not into temptation,
but deliver us from evil:
For Thine is the kingdom, the power and the glory,
for ever and ever.

Matthew 6:9–13

When we work, we work; when we pray, God works.

Selwyn Hughes

He who prays and also works lifts his heart to God with his hands.

St Bernard

The great tragedy of life is not unanswered prayer, but unoffered prayer.

F. B. Myer

You need not cry very loud - He is nearer to us than we think.

Brother Lawrence

Speak to Him thou for He hears, and Spirit with
    Spirit can meet -
Closer is He than breathing, and nearer than
    hands and feet.

Alfred Lord Tennyson

Come near to God and He will come near to you.

James 4:8

We ask what we think is best; God gives what He knows is best.

William Burkitt

Lord of the journey, give me the joy of knowing You are with me every step I take.

Eddie Askew

Keep praying, but be thankful that God's answers are wiser than your prayers.

William Culbertson

Waiting for an answer to prayer is often part of the answer.

John Blanchard

When praying, do not give God instructions - report for duty.

Anon

Satan trembles when he sees the weakest saint upon his knees.

William Cowper

The most direct way to others is always through prayer.

Dietrich Bonhoeffer

Prayer is not the least we can do; it is the most.

John Blanchard

Pray not for lighter burdens, but for stronger backs.

Theodore Roosevelt

Cleanse me from my sin, Lord.
Put thy power within, Lord.
Take me as I am, Lord,
And make me all Thine own.

R. Hudson Pope

If we confess our sins He is faithful and just to forgive us our sins.

1 John 1:9

Thank the Lord because He is good; His love continues for ever.

Psalm 106:1

Teach me, my God and King,
In all things Thee to see,
And what I do in any thing
To do it as for Thee.

George Herbert

To work is to pray.

Benedictine motto

O God, our help in ages past,
Our hope for years to come,
Our shelter from the stormy blast,
And our eternal home.

Isaac Watts

Our help is from the Lord who made the heavens and the earth.

Psalm 124:8

Jesus said: Your heart will be where your treasure is.

Matthew 6:21

May the road rise to meet you.
May the wind be always at your back.
May the sun shine warm upon your face.
May the rains fall softly upon your fields.
Until we meet again may God hold you in the hollow of His hand

Old Gaelic blessing

Prayer girds human weakness with divine strength, turns human folly into heavenly wisdom and gives to troubled mortals the peace of God.

Charles H. Spurgeon

Support us, dear Lord, all the day long, until the shadows lengthen and the evening comes, the busy world is hushed and the fever of life is over and our work done. Then, Lord, in your mercy grant us safe lodging, a holy rest and peace at the last. Amen.

John Henry Newman

PEACE

Jesus said: Peace I leave with you; My peace I give you: I do not give to you as the world gives. Do not let your hearts be troubled.
You believe in God; believe also in Me.

John 14:27

God has said: Never will I leave you; never will I forsake you.

Hebrews 13:5

Jesus said: Let the children come to Me . . . And He put His hands upon them and blessed them.

Mark 10:14 and 16

I know the plans I have for you, declares the Lord:
plans to prosper and not to harm you, plans to
give you hope and a future.

Jeremiah 29:11

Do not be afraid: I will save you; you are Mine.
When you pass through deep waters I will be with
you; your troubles will not overwhelm you.

Isaiah 43:1–2

Thy way not mine, O Lord,
However dark it be,
Lead me by Thine own hand,
Choose out the path for me.

Horatius Bonar

God is able to give us peace when our lives are going to pieces.

James F. Lewis

Jesus said: Peace, be still.

Mark 4:39

Lord, make me an instrument of Thy peace;
Where there is hatred, let me sow love;
Where there is injury, pardon;
Where there is doubt, faith;
Where there is despair, hope;
Where there is darkness, light;
And where there is sadness, joy.

Oh divine Master, grant that I may not so much
    seek
To be consoled as to console;
To be understood as to understand;
To be loved as to love;
For it is in giving that we receive,
It is in pardoning that we are pardoned,
And it is in dying that we are born to eternal life.

St Francis of Assisi

To me You are the sun in June,
The flowers that bloom in May,
The beauty in a quiet time,
The hush at break of day.

To me You are the stars at night
Set in a silver sky,
The lark high up in heavenward flight,
The soft wind's plaintive sigh.

To me You are the firelight glow
That warms and cheers the room,
The softness of the winter's snow,
The lights that banish gloom.

To me You are the soft sweet smell
Of Nature's garden fair,
The cool soft hand that strokes the brow,
Removing stains of care

To me You are the only One,
My charge until my call,
My peace, my tears, my happiness
You are my life, my all.

Leonard C. Crowe

If possible, as far as it lies with you, live at peace with all men.

Romans 12:18

First keep the peace within yourself; then you can also bring peace to others.

Thomas à Kempis

Jesus said: Blessed are the peacemakers, for they shall be called the children of God.

Matthew 5:9

Thou wilt keep him in perfect peace whose mind is stayed on Thee.

Isaiah 26:3

Oh, what peace we often forfeit,
Oh, what needless pain we bear:
All because we do not carry
Everything to God in prayer.

Joseph M. Scriven

The Master is with you wherever you go.

Joshua 1:9

If you look at the world you will be distressed;
If you look within you will be depressed;
If you look at Christ you will be at rest.

Corrie ten Boom

Be of good cheer - I have overcome the world.

John 16:33

Whenever I am afraid I will trust in you.

Psalm 56:3

Do not look forward to what might happen tomorrow – the same everlasting Father who cares for us today will take care of you now and every day. Either He will shield you from suffering or He will give you unfailing strength to bear it. Be at peace, then, and put aside all anxious thoughts and imaginings.

St Francis de Sales

Since the Lord is directing our steps, why try to understand everything that happens along the way?

Proverbs 20:24

Paul said: I have learned the secret of being content - I can do everything through Him who gives me strength.

Philippians 4:12–13

Do not be anxious about anything, but in every situation, by prayer, present your requests to God. And the peace of God will guard your hearts.

Philippians 4:6-7

*Our worst misfortunes never happen . . . most of
our miseries lie in anticipation.*

Charles H. Spurgeon

*Blessed are the single-minded for they shall have
abundance of peace.*

Thomas à Kempis

*Go placidly amid the noise and the haste,
and remember what peace there may be in
silence.*

Max Ehrmann, 'Desiderata'

God be in my head,
And in my understanding;
God be in my eyes,
And in my looking . . .
God be in my heart,
And in my thinking;
God be at my end,
And at my departing.

Sarum Missal

Don't grieve that I have died;
be glad that I have lived.

Child's memorial at
Cricket St Thomas

But all shall be well and all shall be well and all
manner of things shall be well.

Dame Julian of Norwich

The Lord bless you and keep you; the Lord make His face shine upon you and be gracious to you; the Lord turn his face towards you and give you peace.

Numbers 6: 24–26

One thing I ask of the Lord, this is what I seek; that I may dwell in the house of the Lord all the days of my life, to gaze upon the beauty of the Lord and to seek Him in His temple.

Psalm 27:4

The peace of the Lord be always with you.

Book of Common Prayer (Communion)

Drop Thy still dews of quietness
Till all our strivings cease;
Take from our souls the strain and stress,
And let our ordered lives confess
The beauty of Thy peace.

Breathe through the heats of our desire
Thy coolness and Thy balm;
Let sense be dumb, let flesh retire;
Speak through the earthquake, wind and fire,
O still small voice of calm!

John G. Whittier

GUIDANCE

My dearest Lord, be Thou a bright flame before
me; be Thou a guiding star above me; be Thou a
guiding shepherd behind me,
Today and evermore.

St Columba

Turn your eyes upon Jesus –
Look full in His wonderful face
And the things of earth will grow strangely dim
In the light of His glory and grace.

Helen H. Lemmel

Keep Thou my feet; I do not ask to see
The distant scene; one step enough for me.

John Henry Newman

Be bold and be strong! Banish fear and doubt! For remember, the Lord your God is with you wherever you go.

Joshua 1:9

Men give advice;
God gives guidance.

Leonard Ravenhill

Be prepared for God to direct you to something you do not like and teach you to like it.

J. I. Packer

I dare not choose my lot,
I would not if I might;
Choose Thou for me, my God,
So shall I walk aright.

Horatius Bonar

Show me Your way, O Lord; teach me Your paths;
guide me in Your truth and teach me, for You are
God, my Saviour.

Psalm 25:4

Father, I wait Thy daily will;
Thou shalt divide my portion still;
Grant me on earth what seems the best
Till death and heaven reveal the rest.

Isaac Watts

I know not the way God leads me, but well do I know my guide.

Martin Luther

Your world is a lamp to guide me and a light for my path. Open my eyes that I may see wonderful truths in Your law.

Psalm 119:105

The Bible was not given to increase our knowledge, but to change our lives.

D. L. Moody

Wisdom is the right use of knowledge.

Charles H. Spurgeon

There's a time to be silent and a time to speak.

Ecclesiastes 3:7

The tongue has the power of life and death.

Proverbs 18:21

I asked God for strength that I might achieve;
I was made weak that I might learn humbly to
obey.

I asked for health that I might do greater things;
I was given infirmity that I might do better things.

I asked for power that I might have the praise of
men;
I was given weakness that I might face the need
of God.

An unknown soldier in
the American Civil War

How often do we trust each other
And only doubt Our Lord?
We take the words of mortals
Yet distrust His word.
But oh what joy and glory
Would shine on all our days
If we would always remember
God means just what He says.

A. B. Simpson

When God shuts a door He opens a window.

John Ruskin

Whatever is true, whatever is noble, whatever is right, whatever is pure, whatever is lovely, whatever is admirable, if anything is excellent or praiseworthy, think about such things.

Philippians 4:8

God grant me the serenity to accept the things I
*   cannot change,*
Courage to change the things I can,
And wisdom to know the difference.

Reinhold Niebuhr

Going to church doesn't make you a Christian any
more than standing in a garage makes you a car.

Anon

The greatest danger for most of us lies not in
setting our aim too high and falling short, but in
setting our aim too low and achieving our mark.

Michelangelo

There is just enough room in the world for all the people in it, but there is no room for the fences that separate them.

Father Taylor of Boston

There is a sufficiency in the world for man's needs - but not for man's greed.

Mahatma Ghandi

It's not what you have that matters - it is what you do with what you have.

Wilfred Grenfell

Set a guard, O Lord, over my mouth;
keep watch over the door of my lips.

Psalm 141:3

May the words of my mouth and the meditations
of my heart be pleasing in Your sight, my Rock
and my Redeemer.

Psalm 19:14

Lord, speak to me that I may speak in living echoes
of Thy tone.

Frances Ridley Havergal

Don't be afraid, for the Lord will go before you and will be with you; He will not fail nor forsake you.

Deuteronomy 31:8

In all thy ways acknowledge Him, and He shall direct thy paths.

Proverbs 3:6

You can't have everything - where would you put it?

Ann Landes

Look up with wonder,
Look back with gratitude,
Look around with love,
Look within with honesty,
Look ahead with anticipation.

Jim Graham

God is our shelter and our refuge, a timely help in trouble.

Psalm 46:1

You will seek Me and find Me when you seek Me with all your heart.

Jeremiah 29:13

In your anger do not sin - do not let the sun go down while you are still angry. Do not give the devil a foothold.

Ephesians 4:26

When you have completed your daily task go to sleep in peace - God is awake.

Victor Hugo

Commit to the Lord whatever you do, and your plans will succeed.

Proverbs 16:3

Do you not know? Have you not heard? The Lord is the everlasting God, the Creator of the ends of the earth. . . . He gives strength to the weary and increases the power of the weak. . . . Those who hope in the Lord will renew their strength. They will soar on wings like eagles; they will run and not grow weary; they will walk and not be faint.

Isaiah 40: 28–31

When the time of trial comes and all in earth and heaven is dark, and even God's love seems dim: what is there ever left to cling to but the will of the willing heart which says:

> *Father, I know that all my life*
> *Is portioned out for me;*
> *The changes that are sure to come*
> *I do not fear to see;*
> *I ask Thee for a present mind,*
> *Intent on pleasing Thee.*

Henry Drummond

ACTIONS

Christ has no body on earth but yours,
no hands but yours,
no feet but yours.
Yours are the eyes
which must look out at
Christ's compassion
on the world.
Yours are the feet
with which He is to
go about doing good
Yours are the hands
with which He is to
bless men now.

St Teresa of Ávila

Give me the ability to see good things in unexpected places and talents in unexpected people, and give me, O Lord, the grace to tell them so.

From a seventeenth-century Nun's prayer

I expect to pass through this world but once; any good thing therefore that I can do, or any kindness that I can show to any fellow-creature let me do it now; let me not defer or neglect it, for I shall not pass this way again.

Stephen Grellet (an American Quaker)

Attempt great things for God – expect great things from God.

William Carey

The best way to cheer yourself up is to try to cheer up somebody else.

Mark Twain

Never consider whether you are of use – but ever consider you are not your own but His.

Oswald Chambers

Have thy tools ready; God will find thee work.

Charles Kingsley

Do what you can, with what you have, where you are.

Theodore Roosevelt

It is better to wear out than to rust out.

Bishop Richard of Cumberland

Do all the good you can, by all the means you can, in all the ways you can, in all the places you can, at all the times you can, to all the people you can, as long as ever you can.

John Wesley's Motto

If we did the things we were capable of we would astound ourselves.

Thomas Edison

At any given moment you have the power to say – this is not how the story is going to end.

Anon

The dignity of serving God is second only to the dignity of belonging to his family.

John Blanchard

God uses men who are weak and feeble enough to lean on Him.

J. Hudson Taylor

I alone cannot change the world, but I can cast a stone across the water to create many ripples.

Mother Teresa

Find out where you can render a service, then render it. The rest is up to the Lord.

S. S. Kresge

The conduct of our lives is the only proof of the sincerity of our hearts.

Robert Wilson

Modern progress has made the world a neighbourhood, but has given us the task of making it a brotherhood.

Sir Philip Gibbs

Lord give me the grace and strength to blossom where You have planted me.

Margaret Cundiff

Do not be overcome by evil, but overcome evil with good.

Romans 12:21

Oh Lord, dear Lord,
Great Author of the play,
May I in wisdom learn,
The only part that I need play
Is the part that you wrote for me –
The part that You wrote for me.

Joni Eareckson Tada

You will never find time for anything; if you want time you must make it.

Charles Buxton

The man who keeps busy helping the man below him won't have time to be jealous of the man above him.

Henrietta Mears

A rough path is sometimes worth the treading if in so doing we can tread down the brambles in the path of another.

Anon

If God sends us on stony paths, He provides strong shoes.

Corrie ten Boom

He who began a good work in You will carry it on to completion.

Philippians 1:6

There are two ways to get enough - one is to accumulate more and more; the other is to desire less and less.

G. K. Chesterton

I am learning a man can live profoundly without masses of things.

Richard E. Byrd
(after months of solitude in Antarctica)

Kindness is the language which the deaf can hear and the blind can see.

Mark Twain

The only truly happy people are those who have learned how to serve.

Dr Albert Schweitzer

*Who sweeps a room as for Thy laws
Makes that and th' action fine.*

George Herbert

I have strength for anything through Him who gives me power.

Philippians 4:13

Great works do not always lie in our way, but every moment we may do little ones excellently - that is, with great love.

St Francis de Sales

Do not be weary in well-doing.

2 Thessalonians 3:13

If your lips would keep from slips,
Five things observe with care:
Of whom you speak, to whom you speak
And how and when and where.

A wise man

Sympathy is no substitute for action.

David Livingstone

If you walk over the cliff you don't break the law
of gravity - you prove it. In spite of man's misuse
of freewill God is still in control, and sometimes
we have the scars to prove it.

G. K. Chesterton

Two men looked out through bars:
One saw mud - the other saw stars.

Frederick Langbridge

Every good and perfect gift is from above.

James 1:17

Jesus said: Do not worry about tomorrow, for tomorrow will worry about itself - each day has enough trouble of its own.

Matthew 6:34

Worry does not empty tomorrow of its sorrow; it empties today of its strength.

Corrie ten Boom

The problems facing us will not be greater than the power behind us.

Anon

To err is human; to forgive, divine.

Alexander Pope

It always seems impossible until it is done.

Nelson Mandela

We know that in all things God works for the good of those who love Him, who have been called according to His purposes.

Romans 8:28

Jesus said: I tell you the truth, whatever you did for the least of these brothers of Mine you did it for Me.

Matthew 25:40

Jesus said: Come unto Me, all ye that are heavy laden, and I will give you rest.

Matthew 11:28

You haven't lived today until you've done something for someone who can never repay you.

John Bunyan

Let us not grow weary while doing good, for in due season we shall reap a harvest if we do not lose heart.

Galatians 6:9

Christ cared more for humanity than for religion - rather His care for humanity was the chief expression of His religion.

Henry Drummond

Wherever real life is, there Christ goes and He goes there, not only because the great need lies there, but because there is found, so to speak, the raw material with which Christianity works – the life of man.

Henry Drummond

In his heart a man plans his course, but the Lord determines his steps.

Proverbs 16:9

Don't worry about anything; instead, pray about everything: tell God your needs and don't forget to thank Him for His answers.

Philippians 4:6

PRAISE

If music be the food of love, play on.

Shakespeare, Twelfth Night

O come, let us adore Him, Christ the Lord!

Eighteenth-century hymn

Now to the King of all worlds, immortal, invisible, the only God, be honour and glory for ever and ever.

1 Timothy 1:17

We praise thee, O God: we acknowledge thee to be the Lord. All the earth doth worship thee: the Father everlasting.

Book of Common Prayer (Te Deum)

Glory be to God on high and in the earth peace, goodwill towards men.

Book of Common Prayer (Holy Communion)

*Let us with a gladsome mind
Praise the Lord, for He is kind,
For His mercies ay endure,
Ever faithful, ever sure.*

John Milton

Let everything that has breath praise the Lord.

Psalm 150:6

Open my lips, O Lord, that my mouth may proclaim Thy praise.

Psalm 51:15

O all ye works of the Lord, bless ye the Lord: praise Him and magnify Him for ever.

Book of Common Prayer (Benedicite)

So be truly glad! There is wonderful joy ahead, even though the going is rough for a while down here.

1 Peter 1:6

Let all the world in every corner sing,
'My God and King!'

George Herbert

All people that on earth do dwell,
Sing to the Lord with cheerful voice,
Him serve with mirth, His praise forth tell;
Come ye before Him and rejoice.

William Kethe

Music is love in search of a word.

Sidney Lanier

Music strikes in me . . . a profound contemplation
of the First Composer.

Thomas Browne

Composition by L. C. Crowe.

Good night! Good night!
Far flies the light,
But still God's love
Shall flame above,
Making all bright.
Goodnight! Goodnight!

Victor Hugo

Oh, how grateful and thankful I am to the Lord
   because He is so good.
I will sing praise to the name of the Lord who is
   above all lords.

Psalm 7:17

Sing a new song to the Lord! Sing it everywhere
around the world!

Psalm 96:1

Sing to the Lord, O earth! Declare each day that He is the one who saves! Show His glory to the nations! Tell everyone about His miracles, for the Lord is great, and should be highly praised.

1 Chronicles 16:23–5

Sing out your thanks to Him; sing praises to our God, accompanied by harps.

Psalm 147:7

Praise His name with dancing, accompanied by drums and lyre.

Psalm 149:3

I will sing to the Lord as long as I live.
I will praise God to my last breath.

Psalm 104:33

And suddenly there was with the angel a multitude of the heavenly host praising God and saying: Glory to God in the highest, and on earth peace, goodwill toward men.

Luke 2:13–14

ACKNOWLEDGEMENTS

Acknowledgments

Excerpts taken from:

1. **The Holy Bible** – various versions. Scriptures taken from the Holy Bible, New International Version®, NIV®. Copyright © 1973,1978,1984, 2011 by Biblica, Inc.™ Used by permission of Zondervan. All rights reserved worldwide. www.zondervan.com The "NIV" and "New International Version" are trademarks registered in the United States Patent and Trademark Office by Biblica, Inc.™

2. *Complete Gathered Gold*, quotations by John Blanchard – Evangelical Press, Favendale, N. Darlington

3. **United Christian Broadcasters**, Westport Road, Stoke-on-Trent, ST6 4JF

4. **National Christian Trust**, Mulberry House, Chelmsford Road, High Ongar, Essex, CM5 9NL (free issues available from UCB and NCT)

5. **The Leprosy Mission**, Goldhay Way, Orton Goldhay, Peterborough, PE2 5GZ

6. **Hodder & Stoughton Ltd**, Carmelite House, 50 Victoria Embankment, London, EC4Y 0DZ

7. **Faber & Faber Ltd**, Bloomsbury House, 74–77 Great Russell Street, London, WC1B 3DA

Plus various Church and other magazines over several years.

I have enjoyed gathering these quotations over many years and have tried to trace the many sources. I hope that if I have failed to acknowledge these 'borrowed' sources, the people concerned will understand and forgive.